MESSING UP! SPEAKING UP! BUILDING UP!

FEARLESS

THE CONFIDENCE JOURNAL FOR GIRLS

www.stmartins.com
www.castlepointbooks.com

The Castle Point Books trademark is owned by Castle Point Publishing, LLC.
Castle Point books are published and distributed by St. Martin's Press.

ISBN 978-1-250-21404-1 (trade paperback)

Design by Joanna Williams

Images used under license by Shutterstock.com

Our books may be purchased in bulk for promotional, educational,
or business use. Please contact your local bookseller or the Macmillan
Corporate and Premium Sales Department at 1-800-221-7945,
extension 5442, or by email at MacmillanSpecialMarkets@macmillan.com.

First Edition: July 2019

10 9 8 7 6 5 4 3 2 1

MESSING UP! SPEAKING UP! BUILDING UP!

FEARLESS

THE
CONFIDENCE JOURNAL
FOR GIRLS

JENNIFER CALVERT

Castle Point Books
NEW YORK

"IT TAKES **COURAGE** TO GROW UP AND **BECOME** WHO YOU REALLY ARE."

—E. E. CUMMINGS

It's natural to be afraid, to hesitate, to think before you act. After all, bounding fearlessly toward a cliff's edge could end badly. Instead, being fearless means being afraid but moving forward with the confidence that you can handle what lies ahead. You walk toward the cliff, armed with a parachute and a plan for whatever you find beyond it.

Confidence turns thought into action. It's the difference between seizing an opportunity and letting it pass you by, between succeeding and not even trying. Without confidence, we stop ourselves before we even start. We turn back because we think we're not good enough to face the challenges ahead.

But you *are* good enough. You have everything you need to overcome obstacles. Confidence just helps you realize it. The best part is, you don't need to be naturally fearless to tap into it. Confidence is a skill like any other—the more you practice it, the stronger it gets.

The quotes and prompts in this journal are designed to help you practice. As you complete each exercise, you'll begin to recognize your strengths and build the confidence you need to bring them into the world. Work through the pages at your own pace, and don't worry about being perfect or doing it "right." Just go for it!

Being underestimated by someone is super frustrating, especially when talking back can get you into trouble. So, vent your frustration here. Have you ever been put down by someone more powerful than you? What did you really want to say that you couldn't at the time?

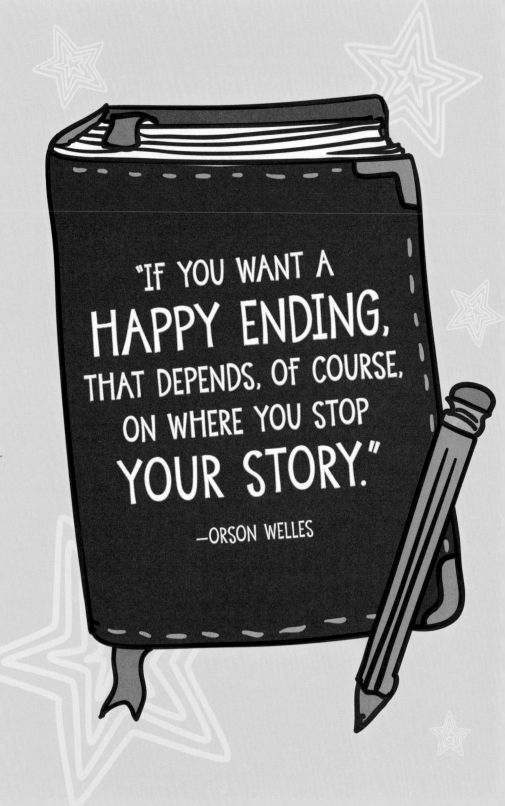

If you wrote a book about your life so far, what genre would it be in? Comedy? Adventure? Sci-fi? What does the rest of your story look like? (Don't forget the plot twists!)

"CHOOSE PEOPLE
WHO LIFT YOU UP."

—MICHELLE OBAMA

They say you are the average of the five people you spend the most time with. Are there any toxic, unkind, or negative people in your life you need to let go of to bring your average up?

"IT'S THE LITTLE THINGS
THAT MAKE HAPPY MOMENTS,
NOT THE GRAND EVENTS.
JOY COMES IN SIPS,
NOT GULPS."

—SHARON DRAPER

No matter how bad your day is,

you can always find a handful of little things that lift your spirits. Try this: Set a timer for one minute and list ten tiny things that put a smile on your face before the bell rings. (Tip: Don't overthink it!)

1. _____

2. _____

3. _____

4. _____

5. _____

6. _____

7. _____

8. _____

9. _____

10. _____

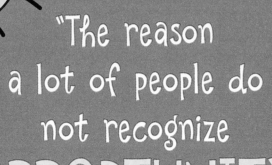

"The reason
a lot of people do
not recognize
OPPORTUNITY
is because it
usually goes around
wearing overalls
looking like
HARD WORK."

—THOMAS EDISON

Thomas Edison invented the light bulb after a thousand failed attempts.

Can you imagine if he'd given up after just a few? Have you ever succeeded at something after failing at it first? Is there anything you'd like to try again, just one more time?

"LIFE'S CHALLENGES
are not supposed to paralyze you,
they're supposed to help you
DISCOVER WHO YOU ARE."

 —BERNICE JOHNSON REAGON

Every video game has its share of bosses you need to beat before you can move forward. What is it that's standing in your way right now? What's your strategy for leveling up?

"THERE IS NO SUNRISE SO BEAUTIFUL THAT IT IS WORTH WAKING ME UP TO SEE IT."

—MINDY KALING

There's no "right" time to wake up—

except maybe on school days. The world is made up of early birds, night owls, and everything in between.

When do you feel most awake? What's your favorite thing about that time of day (or night)?

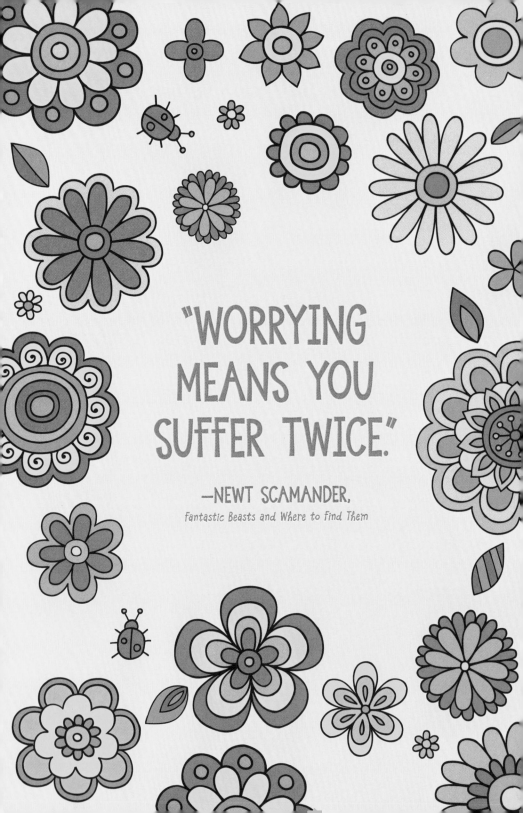

"WORRYING MEANS YOU SUFFER TWICE."

—NEWT SCAMANDER,
Fantastic Beasts and Where to Find Them

Freaking out about something that hasn't even happened yet means missing out on all the fun you could be having right this minute. What's something you've been worrying about? Let it out here, then decide whether you can let it go. If you can't, what can you do to breathe easier?

"I WANT MORE
GiRLS' NiGHTS,
MORE DiNNER PARTiES,
MORE DATE NiGHTS,
MORE NiGHTS ON THE COUCH
WITH ZUCCHiNi FRiES WATCHING
BAD REALITY TELEVISION."

—CHRiSSY TEiGEN

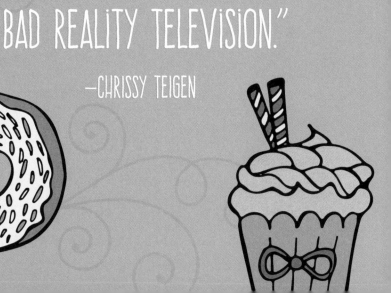

Some of the best things in Life are the little, everyday things we take for granted. What do you want more of in your life?

"WE JUST NEED TO BE
KINDER TO OURSELVES.
IF WE TREATED OURSELVES
THE WAY WE TREATED OUR BEST
FRIEND, CAN YOU IMAGINE HOW MUCH
BETTER OFF WE WOULD BE?"

—MEGHAN MARKLE

Who are three of your favorite people to be around?

1. _____

2. _____

3. _____

When they're feeling down, what do you do or say to help them back up?

_____

_____

_____

_____

_____

_____

_____

_____

_____

_____

What's your favorite way to play?

Circle the creative things you like to do, and add any that are missing!

Write stories

Read stories

Put on plays

Paint

Draw

Craft

Find shapes in clouds

Build Lego creations

Make a scrapbook

Create collages

Invent new recipes

Tell ghost stories

Put on a puppet show

Build a fort

Plant a garden

Build a birdhouse

Design clothing

Write songs

Play music

Make jewelry

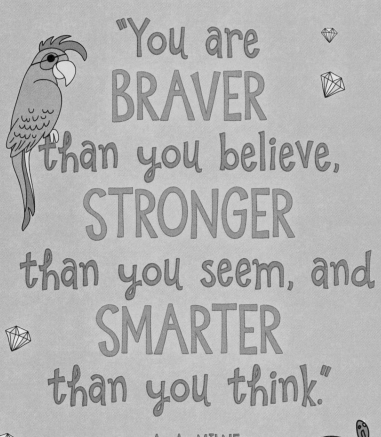

"You are
BRAVER
than you believe,
STRONGER
than you seem, and
SMARTER
than you think."

—A. A. MILNE

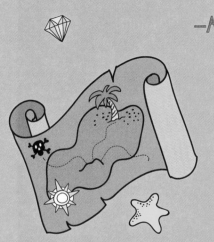

When you focus on what could go wrong, you forget about all the things that can go right. Think back to the last time you were really afraid to do something. What were you afraid of? How did it turn out?

List your top five favorite movies.

1. _____

2. _____

3. _____

4. _____

5. _____

Do they have anything in common?

What makes them better than all the others that might have made the list?

"Don't ever hear in your own head, 'Who am I to say something?' You are a human being! You are a person! YOU CAN 100% CHANGE THE WORLD. And it's small ways, it's everyday ways, it's the little things that count. BE BRAVE."

—EMMA WATSON

If you show the same problem to a hundred people, you could end up with a hundred different solutions. Everyone has something different or unique to contribute. Big or small, what would you change if you could? How would you do it differently?

"IF I DON'T POKE MY HEAD
OUT OF MY SHELL
AND SHOW PEOPLE WHO I AM,
ALL ANYONE WILL EVER THINK
I AM IS MY SHELL."

—SHONDA RHIMES

When it comes to letting people in on the real you, it's normal to feel a little shy or awkward. But sharing what makes you you can lead to great things, like close friendships and new opportunities.

What are the top three things you wish more people knew about you? (These could be things you're good at, places you want to travel to, or even secrets you've never told anyone.)

1. _____

_____

_____

2. _____

_____

_____

3. _____

_____

_____

How can you help people learn more about you?

"MAKING WORDS RHYME FOR A LIVING IS ONE OF THE GREAT JOYS OF MY LIFE.... THAT'S A SUPERPOWER I'VE BEEN VERY CONSCIOUS OF DEVELOPING. I STARTED AT THE SAME LEVEL AS EVERYBODY ELSE, AND THEN I JUST LISTENED TO MORE MUSIC AND TALKED TO MYSELF UNTIL IT WAS AN ACTUAL SUPERPOWER I COULD PULL OUT ON SPECIAL OCCASIONS."

—LIN-MANUEL MIRANDA

What's your superpower? Even if it's not at super strength just yet, what's a skill or a hobby you want to develop? What are some ways you can make it happen?

"OUR SIMILARITIES BRING US TO A COMMON GROUND; OUR DIFFERENCES ALLOW US TO BE FASCINATED BY EACH OTHER."

—TOM ROBBINS

Do you and your bestie share a brain?

From inside jokes to favorite ice cream combinations, it's great to have someone who totally gets you. But friendship isn't just about what you have in common—it's also about how you complement each other.

Go through the list of traits below and write your initials next to any that describe you, and your BFF's initials next to any that describe them. Circle the ones you have in common.

_____ Funny
_____ Witty
_____ Smart
_____ Athletic
_____ Open
_____ Outgoing
_____ Shy
_____ Patient
_____ Responsible
_____ Adventurous
_____ Kind
_____ Social
_____ Spontaneous
_____ Thoughtful
_____ Optimistic
_____ Anxious
_____ Energetic
_____ Honest

_____ Adaptable
_____ Passionate
_____ Confident
_____ Brave
_____ Loyal
_____ Determined
_____ Studious
_____ Stubborn
_____ Charming
_____ Helpful
_____ Independent
_____ Encouraging
_____ Reasonable
_____ Trustworthy
_____ Creative
_____ Humble
_____ Observant

"THOSE WHO DON'T JUMP
WILL NEVER FLY."

—LEENA AHMAD ALMASHAT

It's not always the big leaps that make your stomach do somersaults.

Even the little, everyday things, like giving a presentation at school or joining a new club, can seem scary.

What's got your stomach in knots? How can you help yourself feel better about making the jump?

"BEAUTY BEGINS
THE MOMENT
YOU DECIDE TO BE
YOURSELF."

—COCO CHANEL

Our favorite things about a person are often the things that make them a little different from everybody else, whether that's a silly, contagious laugh or a love of vintage threads.

Write down five weird and wonderful ways you stand out from the crowd.

1.

2.

3.

4.

5.

"Always be on the lookout for the presence of **WONDER.**"

—E. B. WHITE

Following our curiosity can lead us to discover new adventures, opportunities, and even career paths. What person, place, or thing is piquing your curiosity the most right now? What about it makes you want to know more?

"YOU ARE CAPABLE OF
MORE THAN YOU KNOW."

—GLINDA THE GOOD WITCH

We all have that voice in our heads

at times telling us we *can't* do something. It trots out all of our mistakes and insecurities as proof and makes us afraid to move forward. Today, it's time to break up with the Vicious Voice. Write it a letter telling it how wrong it was to underestimate you, then kick it to the curb!

"NO ONE
LOOKS STUPID
WHEN THEY'RE
HAVING FUN."

—AMY POEHLER

**Think about all the times you did
something goofy** and hilarious with friends. Write
about your favorite here, including all the juicy details! What
made that moment great?

"THE BEST THING ONE
CAN DO WHEN IT'S RAINING
IS TO LET IT RAIN."

—HENRY WADSWORTH LONGFELLOW

When things go wrong, it's okay to wallow for a little bit. Letting yourself feel sad, hurt, angry, or annoyed can help you process what happened so you can move forward. Use this space to free-write about what you're feeling.

"You get in life
what you have the
COURAGE
to ask for."

—OPRAH WINFREY

When you want something badly enough, you might find yourself wishing for it on every shooting star, birthday candle, and dandelion puff. Label the seeds below with the things you want most right now.

"THE WORLD IS FULL OF WONDERFUL THINGS YOU HAVEN'T SEEN YET. DON'T EVER GIVE UP ON THE CHANCE OF SEEING THEM."

—J. K. ROWLING

Plan a grand adventure! Where are you going? Who's going with you? What will you eat? Use your imagination and include as much detail as possible.

"LIFE IS LIKE RIDING A BICYCLE. TO KEEP YOUR BALANCE YOU MUST KEEP MOVING."

—ALBERT EINSTEIN

Whether you woke up on the wrong side of the bed or something specific sparked your bad mood, shifting your focus can help you snap out of it. Moving your body can be an especially great way to get out of your head. What are five fun or distracting things you could get up and do right now?

1.

2.

3.

4.

5.

When you overthink things, you can sometimes stop yourself before you even have a chance to start. What's something you've accomplished even though you thought it was impossible at first?

"TO BE CLEAR,
I'M HAPPY
TO DO THE DISHES,
BUT THERE'S NO UNIVERSE
IN WHICH I GENERATE
DINNER."

—CRISTINA YANG, *GREY'S ANATOMY*

You have to say "no" to some things

so you can make room for others—the ones you really enjoy. Understanding your strengths and weaknesses makes that a lot easier. List them here, and don't be afraid to be honest with yourself. No one is good at everything, but no one is bad at everything, either!

Strengths	Weaknesses

"THE SECRET OF
GREAT STYLE IS
TO FEEL GOOD IN
WHAT YOU WEAR."

—INÈS DE LA FRESSANGE

Whether it's a beat-up tee featuring your favorite band or a perfectly tailored dress, our favorite clothes have the power to change our whole outlook. Which outfit or accessory helps you feel comfortable? Joyful? Unstoppable? Why do you think it does that?

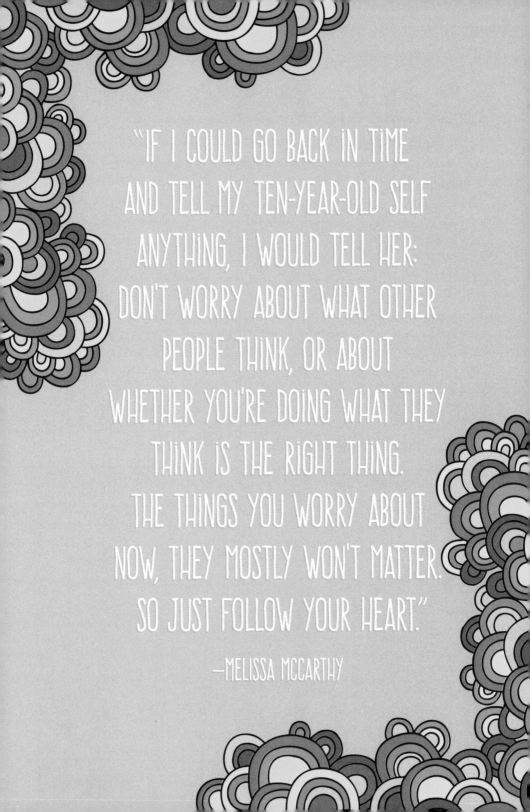

"IF I COULD GO BACK IN TIME AND TELL MY TEN-YEAR-OLD SELF ANYTHING, I WOULD TELL HER: DON'T WORRY ABOUT WHAT OTHER PEOPLE THINK, OR ABOUT WHETHER YOU'RE DOING WHAT THEY THINK IS THE RIGHT THING. THE THINGS YOU WORRY ABOUT NOW, THEY MOSTLY WON'T MATTER. SO JUST FOLLOW YOUR HEART."

—MELISSA MCCARTHY

Imagine that ten years have gone by.

Write a letter from your future self letting you know how everything turns out. Make sure you include plenty of specifics, such as where you live, what you've accomplished, what your friends are like, and anything else you can think of.

"I TRIED FOR A
SHORT TIME TO BE
SOMETHING I WASN'T,
AND HAD NO SUCCESS
WITH IT. IT'S A
PRACTICAL SOLUTION
TO JUST BE YOURSELF."

—KATE MCKINNON

There's a difference between stretching to expand your comfort zone (something you do for *you*) and pretending to be someone you're not (something you do for others). When someone pressures you to look or act a certain way, how do you respond? How do you *want* to respond?

"IF YOU FEEL LIKE A WEIRDO,
IT'S OKAY, BECAUSE
WEIRDOS RULE
THE WORLD."

—AUBREY PLAZA

Think about all of the successful people you know—parents, teachers, distant relatives, or even celebrities. Are any of them dorky, nerdy, goofy, or weird? Try to think of at least five and list them below.

1. _____

Their Success | Their Quirks

2. _____

Their Success | Their Quirks

3. _____

Their Success | Their Quirks

4. _____

Their Success | Their Quirks

5. _____

Their Success | Their Quirks

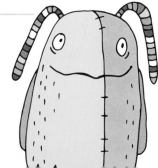

"The whole
BEAUTY OF MUSIC
is that it goes
where your words
won't let you."

—Anne Hathaway

Imagine your life as a movie, then create a soundtrack to match. Be sure to include songs you love for all the plot points—the highs and the lows, the joy and the pain.

1.

2.

3.

4.

5.

6.

7.

8.

9.

10.

11.

12.

"Somewhere along the way, someone is going to tell you, 'There is no *I* in team.' What you should tell them is, 'Maybe not. But there is an *I* in independence, individuality, and integrity.'"

—George Carlin

Some people thrive on collaboration

while others crave time to themselves. Which works better for you: being part of a team, or doing your own thing? Maybe you need a little of both. Why?

"WE KEEP MOVING FORWARD,
OPENING NEW DOORS,
AND DOING NEW THINGS,
BECAUSE WE'RE

CURIOUS

AND CURIOSITY KEEPS LEADING
US DOWN NEW PATHS."

—WALT DISNEY

Maybe you've always known you wanted to be a world-class violinist

or a champion tennis player. But most of the time, the only way to figure out whether you'll enjoy doing something is to give it a try.

Go through the list below and put a star next to the things you want to try, an X next to the things you don't, and a question mark next to the ones you're not quite sure about. And if you see any you absolutely hate, go ahead and scribble them out!

___ Horseback riding
___ Choir
___ **Sports**
___ Theater
___ Science club
___ Dance
___ Cheer
___ **Band**
___ Boy Scouts or
     Girls Scouts
___ Creative writing
___ Art

___ **Coding**
___ Photography
___ Book club
___ Languages
___ **Woodworking**
___ Volunteering
___ 4-H
___ Knitting or crochet
___ **Pottery**
___ Debate club
___ Robotics

Is something missing? Add it here:

_____ _____

_____ _____

_____ _____

"THERE WILL ALWAYS BE PEOPLE
WHO ARE MUCH BETTER AT
DOING THIS OR DOING THAT—
BUT YOU ARE THE ONLY YOU."

—NEIL GAIMAN

Sometimes we need reminders that we're pretty great. Write an encouraging song, poem, story, rap, or cheer that you can look at whenever you need help remembering how awesome you are.

"I SAW THAT
MY LIFE WAS A
VAST GLOWING
EMPTY PAGE
AND I COULD DO
ANYTHING
I WANTED."

—JACK KEROUAC

Your story awaits! What are the top five things you want to do or accomplish in your lifetime?

1.

2.

3.

4.

5.

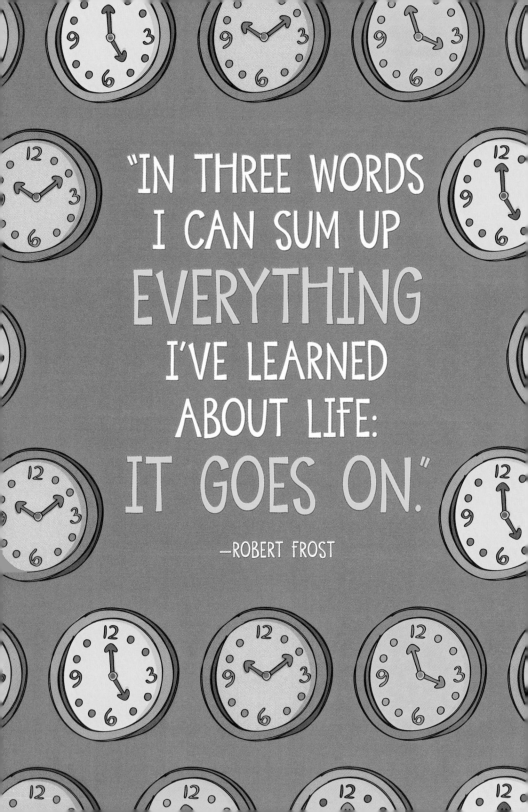

"IN THREE WORDS
I CAN SUM UP
EVERYTHING
I'VE LEARNED
ABOUT LIFE:
IT GOES ON."

—ROBERT FROST

When you're feeling overwhelmed,

it can be hard to tell what really matters from what doesn't. Every little change, choice, and embarrassment can make you feel like the sky is falling. The next time something's really weighing on your mind, come to this page and answer these three questions to help you figure out whether it's worth worrying about:

"DECISIONS
ARE MADE BY THOSE
WHO SHOW UP."

—AARON SORKIN

What area of your life do you wish you had a little more control over?

Are there any small ways that you can take control or participate more in that area? If you hate taking the bus, maybe you can bring a good book and turn that twenty minutes into "me time." If you don't like how the chores are divided up at home, maybe you can come up with an alternative that works better for everyone.

"I LOVE RULES AND I LOVE FOLLOWING THEM, UNLESS THAT RULE IS STUPID."

—ANNA KENDRICK

Not all rules are created equal.

Can you think of any rules that just don't make sense to you?
How would you change them?

"WHERE YOU ARE RIGHT NOW DOESN'T HAVE TO DETERMINE WHERE YOU END UP."

—PRESIDENT BARACK OBAMA

Life can turn on a dime, especially when you make the choice to make a change. What would you like to change about your life? What's a teeny tiny step you can take right now in the direction of that change?

"BE OPEN TO LEARNING
NEW LESSONS,
EVEN IF THEY
CONTRADICT THE
LESSONS YOU LEARNED
YESTERDAY."

—ELLEN DEGENERES

Keeping an open mind gives you the flexibility to change it and the opportunity to be amazed. What are three things you've learned that totally blew your mind?

1. _____

2. _____

3. _____

Come back and add to this page whenever you learn something new that surprises you.

_____
_____
_____
_____
_____
_____
_____
_____
_____
_____
_____
_____

"WHAT WE SAY TO OURSELVES
IN THE PRIVACY OF
OUR OWN MINDS,
MATTERS. IT DRIVES OUR BEHAVIOR,
WHICH DRIVES OUR DESTINY,
WHICH SHAPES OUR WORLD."

—MARIE FORLEO

About sixty thousand thoughts run through your mind every day. If they're mostly negative, you're not going to have a very good day. So fill this page with all the fears, criticisms, and worry that have been taking up space in your brain lately. Then destroy them—scribble them out, paint a picture over them.

"We just need to be kind,
UNCONDITIONALLY
and without ulterior motive,
even—or rather, especially—
when we'd prefer not to be."

—JOSH RADNOR

The great thing about kindness is that even the tiniest bit of it has the power to affect everyone around it—the person giving it, the person receiving it, and anyone who sees it. Is there an act of kindness that stands out in your mind?

"IT IS IMPOSSIBLE FOR YOU TO BE ANGRY AND LAUGH AT THE SAME TIME. ANGER AND LAUGHTER ARE MUTUALLY EXCLUSIVE AND YOU HAVE THE POWER TO CHOOSE EITHER."

—WAYNE DYER

When was the last time you laughed so hard your stomach hurt? What made you laugh?

"JUMP AND YOU
WILL FIND OUT
HOW TO UNFOLD
YOUR WINGS
AS YOU FALL."

—RAY BRADBURY

Even the most detailed plans can only take you so far. Are you a natural—born planner or someone who goes with the flow? Can you think of a time when Plan B worked out even better than Plan A?

"YOU KNOW, A DOG CAN SNAP YOU OUT OF ANY KIND OF **BAD MOOD** THAT YOU'RE IN FASTER THAN YOU CAN THINK OF."

—JILL ABRAMSON

They say, "Fake it 'til you make it," but sometimes it's hard to smile for the camera if you're not feeling it. The trick is to think about things that genuinely make you happy, which will instantly boost your mood and make you smile for real.

List the top three things that bring a smile to your face, then remember them the next time you need a dose of instant happiness.

1.

2.

3.

"WITH FREEDOM,
BOOKS, FLOWERS,
AND THE MOON,
WHO COULD NOT
BE HAPPY?"

—OSCAR WILDE

A little sunshine can do a world of good. Grab this journal, go sit in the grass, and write down all the little things you notice about the great outdoors. (Hate nature? Write about that!)

"YOU CAN'T ALWAYS CHOOSE
WHAT HAPPENS TO YOU,
BUT YOU CAN ALWAYS CHOOSE
HOW YOU FEEL ABOUT IT."

—DANIELLE LAPORTE

How do you want to feel today?

Choose one feeling from the list below and circle it. Check in with yourself throughout the day and see whether you can find opportunities to feel this way. (You can come back to this exercise and circle a new word whenever you want!)

Expansive	Courageous	Valued
Engaged	Energized	Loved
Joyful	Grateful	Appreciated
Encouraged	Strong	Ready
Compassionate	Free	Unstoppable
Lighthearted	Graceful	Brilliant
Seen	Connected	Insightful
Heard	Beautiful	Open
Comfortable	Flowing	Resilient
Peaceful	Powerful	Loyal
Empowered	Safe	Attentive
Inspired	Vibrant	Patient
Bold	Loving	Optimistic
Supported	Grounded	Useful
Abundant	Nourished	Clear
Authentic	Creative	Independent
Magical	Adventurous	Spontaneous
Playful	Exuberant	Fierce

"The best things happen by accident—and those end up being

THE MAGIC.

Every time I've followed my gut, it's been better than when I've tried to do what I was supposed to do."

—Zooey Deschanel

Sometimes your gut knows better than your brain does. Can you remember a time when you just *knew* what to do, even if you don't know how you knew?

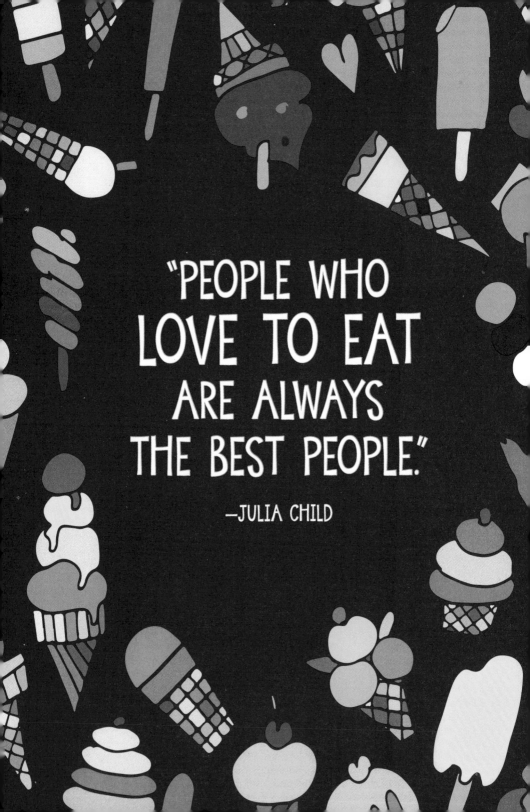

"PEOPLE WHO LOVE TO EAT ARE ALWAYS THE BEST PEOPLE."

—JULIA CHILD

Through smell, taste, and shared experiences, food has the power to connect us with some of our best memories. What are the three most delicious things you've ever eaten? Where were you and what were you doing when you enjoyed them?

1.

2.

3.

"WHAT I'M LOOKING FOR IS A BLESSING NOT IN DISGUISE."

—JEROME K. JEROME

It's normal to be disappointed when things don't work out the way you'd hoped. If you're lucky, that temporary disappointment leads to something better— a "blessing in disguise." For example, you arrive too late to choir practice to sit next to your crush, so you sit next to a girl who ends up becoming your best friend. (And that crush turns out to be kind of a jerk, anyway.)

Has there ever been a time when things didn't go the way you expected them to, but instead worked out even better?

"YOU WANT TO COME HOME
TO A NICE FIRM BED WITH THE
CORNERS TUCKED IN SO YOU
START OVER, LIKE EACH NIGHT
IS LIKE A NEW NIGHT."

—GABRIELLE UNION

Little rituals can help us feel ready to face the day or wind down from it. Do you have a daily ritual? Maybe it's making your bed in the morning or treating yourself to something sweet after school. What does this ritual mean to you?

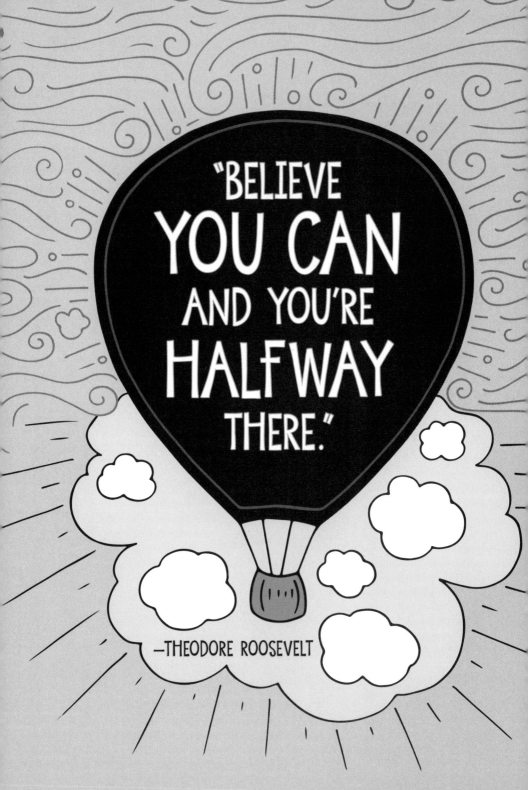

Sometimes, the only things holding us back are our own beliefs.

What's something that you really want to do, but you keep finding reasons to put it off?

Fill the bubbles with those reasons—big and intimidating, silly and small—then imagine popping each one!

"I'VE LEARNED THAT PEOPLE
WILL FORGET WHAT YOU SAID,
PEOPLE WILL FORGET WHAT YOU DID,
BUT PEOPLE WILL NEVER FORGET
HOW YOU MADE THEM FEEL."

—MAYA ANGELOU

How do you think you make the people around you feel?

How would you like them to feel when they're around you?

Are the answers to both questions the same?

"YOU CAN BE A GOOD PERSON WITH A KIND HEART AND STILL SAY *NO*."

—LORI DESCHENE

Are you a people pleaser, a boundary-setting boss, or something in between? Which people or situations do you wish you could say "no" to? Which people or situations do you wish you could say "yes" to?

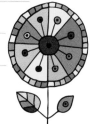

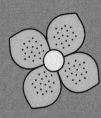

"IT TOOK ME QUITE
A LONG TIME TO DEVELOP
A VOICE, AND NOW THAT
I HAVE IT, I AM NOT
GOING TO BE SILENT."

—MADELEINE ALBRIGHT

We've all been there: someone says something hurtful or annoying and you spend the rest of the day stewing about it and coming up with the perfect response. Think back to the last time it happened. What did you want to say?

If you could go back in time, would you actually say it?

"I have insecurities, of course, but I DON'T HANG OUT with anybody who points them out to me."

—ADELE

Everyone battles insecurities, but you should never let them stop you from appreciating the things that make you unique. List *at least three* things you love about the way you look. They can be as little as the freckle on your chin or the polish on your toes—as long as it makes you happy!

1. _____

2. _____

3. _____

_____

_____

_____

_____

_____

_____

_____

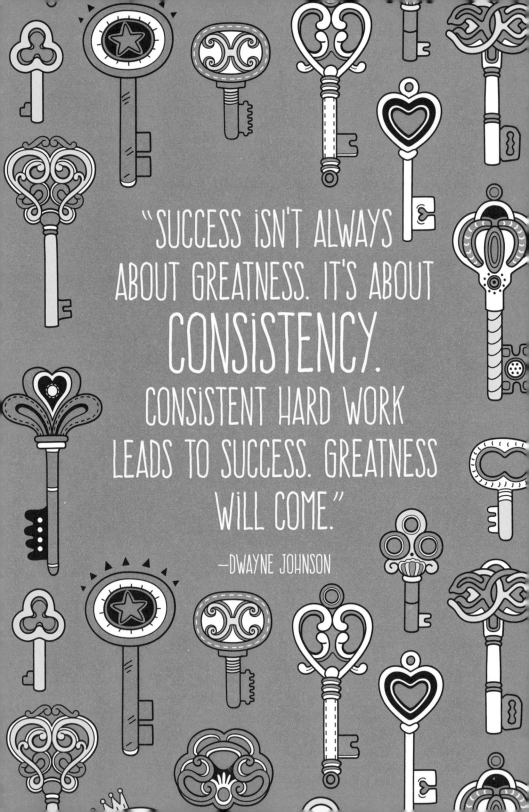

"SUCCESS ISN'T ALWAYS ABOUT GREATNESS. IT'S ABOUT CONSISTENCY. CONSISTENT HARD WORK LEADS TO SUCCESS. GREATNESS WILL COME."

—DWAYNE JOHNSON

List all of the things you're really good at.

Put a star next to the ones you had to work hard for, and a check next to the ones that come naturally to you. Now circle the things you really enjoy doing. Notice any overlap?

"LIFE IS ABOUT USING THE WHOLE BOX OF CRAYONS."

—RUPAUL

Next to each color below, write down how that color makes you feel. Circle the good ones, then try to incorporate more of those colors into your life whenever you can. Buy a pack of plum-colored pens or a cobalt-blue phone case—whatever makes you smile!

Red _____

Denim _____

Maroon _____

Periwinkle _____

Scarlet _____

Indigo _____

Brick _____

Violet _____

Burnt orange _____

Lavender _____

Lilac _____

Coral _____

Apricot _____

Purple _____

Tangerine _____

Fuchsia _____

Orange _____

Hot pink _____

Canary yellow _____

Rose _____

Butter yellow _____

Berry _____

Blush _____

Chartreuse _____

Beige _____

Green _____

Brown _____

Olive _____

Black _____

Forest green _____

Robin's egg blue _____

Gray _____

Aquamarine _____

Gold _____

Teal _____

Silver _____

Turquoise _____

Brass _____

Sky blue _____

Rose gold _____

Cobalt blue _____

Copper _____

"WHAT LITTLE BIT
CAN I DO?
WHOSE LIFE CAN
I TOUCH?"

—PRIYANKA CHOPRA

Who can you think of that is making a difference in the world in a way that you admire? It can be anyone—someone you saw on the news, on social media, on TV, or in your life. What about them would you like to emulate in your own life?